EVERYTHING BARREN WILL BE BLESSED

Also by
Don Thompson

Back Roads
Where We Live
Sittin' On Grace Slick's Stoop
Turning Sixty
Been There Done That

Everything Barren Will Be Blessed

Poems by
Don Thompson

PINYON PUBLISHING
Montrose, Colorado

Copyright © 2012 by Don Thompson

All rights reserved. Except as permitted under the U.S. Copyright Act of 1976, no part of this publication may be reproduced, distributed, or transmitted in any form or by any means, or stored in a database or retrieval system, without the prior written permission of the publisher, except for brief quotations in articles, books, and reviews.

Cover Painting by Susan E. Elliott

Photograph of Don Thompson by Chris Thompson

First Edition: March 2012

Pinyon Publishing
23847 V66 Trail, Montrose, CO 81403
www.pinyon-publishing.com

Library of Congress Control Number: 2012934039
ISBN: 978-1-936671-06-9

Acknowledgments

Some of these poems, often in earlier versions, appeared in the following publications: *Albatross, Avocet, California Quarterly, Haruah, Nomad's Choir, Penwood, Plainsongs, Roanoke Review, Ruminate, Slant, Time of Singing, Xavier Review.*

The difference between Patrick's magic and the magic of the druids is that in Patrick's world all beings and events come from the hand of God, who loves human beings and wishes them success. And though that success is of an ultimate kind—and, therefore, does not preclude suffering—all nature, indeed the whole of the created universe, conspires to mankind's good, teaching, succoring, saving.

—Thomas Cahill, *How the Irish Saved Civilization*

Contents

I

Old Coyote (1)   3

Water   4

Buena Vista Slough (1)   5

Spicer City Market   6

Preacher Valley   7

Pistachio Grove (1)   8

Tumbleweeds   9

Crow   10

Hawk (1)   11

Egret (1)   12

Almond Grove (1)   13

Quaking Aspen   14

When The Drought Ended   15

Bear Mountain After Rain   16

Urban Redwoods   17

Time (1)   18

Peace (1)   19

Lights out   20

II

Ojai Fire, 2006   25

Weeds (1)   26

Wrong Turn   27

Old Coyote (2)   28

Time (2)   30

Kern River Canal   31

Reservoir   32

Moths   33

Seed   34

Lizards   35

Buena Vista Slough (2)   36

After Midnight   37

Weeds (2)   38

Flat Earth   39

Egret (2)   40

Peace (2)   41

III

Kern National Wildlife Reserve 45

Ancestors 46

Peace (3) 47

Penman Springs Road 48

Buena Vista Slough (3) 49

Old Road 50

Abandoned Labor Camp 51

Hawk (2) 52

Dove Season 53

October 54

Almond Grove (2) 55

Unfair 56

December 57

Pistachio Grove (2) 58

Snow On Elk Hills 60

Strangers 61

Downstream 62

I

OLD COYOTE (1)

An old coyote alone in the fog,
somehow lost where he lives,
looking over his shoulder
in a way we all recognize,

seems made of thin fog himself,
almost transparent, simultaneously
assuming his familiar form
as he vanishes.

This is just a moment, I know,
in a long, uncertain life
—nowhere near long enough—
that also comes as it goes.

But it holds. It holds.
Coyote and I stand here,
two ghosts who cling to our bones,
trying hard not to fade.

WATER

Everything here reminds us of water—
to have or have not:

sky like an empty bowl, useless
because of the contrail crack in it;

trees along the slough—
a long line of dusty refugees

with nowhere to go, some dying,
some dead, some too stubborn to perish;

knee-deep alfalfa thriving
on one side of the road and on the other,

the dun, done-for, bare dirt
with a scattering of anonymous scrub—

and no difference between the two fields
except water.

BUENA VISTA SLOUGH (1)

In less than one square mile from here,
so many birds are singing, unheard,
that if each note weighed an ounce,
their songs would add up to tons.

Not to mention incessant insect chatter—
hiss and buzz and crackle like fire.
If we could hear that, we'd think
the whole world is burning.

And maybe it is …
That invisible conflagration could be
the light we see by
when we close our eyes in the dark.

And maybe it's all the birds singing,
that inaudible ballast,
not gravity, that holds us down
so we don't drift away from ourselves.

SPICER CITY MARKET

The crossroads store is open again,
probably not for long,
whitewashed over the old grime.

The new owner has parked in front
like a customer,
but no one is taking the bait.

Though the door is propped open,
it's dark inside, disconcerting,
and you just know

everything in stock is stale or sour—
schemes and false starts, hope
long past its expiration date.

PREACHER VALLEY

Everything we need to know
has been written in unhurried longhand
between the hills and the sky.
You can trace it with your finger.

It's all carved in stone, too,
in those jagged musings of freeze and thaw.
Cottonwood and scrub oak
have been pinned to the earth like memos.

It's even written for us
in the crabbed scrawl of the grass
and the scribbles of tumbleweed—
forever irritated, impatient

because we never notice
and go around muttering discontent,
self-obsessed and oblivious
as if our hearts were illiterate.

PISTACHIO GROVE (1)

The nut trees are still bare and gray,
as if they can't shake off
the bad memories of a long winter.

They must be old,
down to their last harvest—
if they can manage to blossom soon.

But it's not all their fault.
When spring finally arrives here,
it has nothing much to offer:

grass that never had a chance,
drying out already,
and a smudge of mustard on the hills.

TUMBLEWEEDS

A lost tribe of tumbleweeds
crosses the road
a half mile or so ahead of me,
bounding along
while little ones hustle to keep up.

They're uprooted, of course,
subject to the wind's whims,
and could end anywhere—
maybe against a fence
to be gathered and burned by farm hands.

I know that …
But they seem so cheerful,
confidant and in control,
as if pulling the wind behind them
caught on thousands of tiny hooks.

CROW

Crows never make excuses,
unlike us—but like us
complain bitterly about their blessings.

This one beside the road,
dissatisfied with the leftover rabbit
I killed for him yesterday,

squawks at the cosmos without thinking,
anymore than we do,
how easy life is for him—

compared to rabbits, so undemanding,
for whom every run is a risk
neither man nor crow would take.

HAWK (1)

An indistinct glittering in the road
turns out to be the wing of a dead hawk
lifted to catch the sun.

One miscalculation, a glitch
of mere inches killed him—
inches that keep everyone alive

for awhile. I think
of that elegant, austere soul,
those eyes too keen for comfort,

flying forever into the light,
and I swerve like a small bird
to miss him.

EGRET (1)

Now the consummate egret descends
on an alfalfa field—huge,
its wingspan as wide as a sheet
fluttering on a clothesline,
and all at once I know
precisely what white was meant to be.

By comparison, snow pales.
A welder's arc would dim
to a votive glow, and lightning
would be less than a wet fuse
next to such scintillation—

which lasts for as much of forever
as a few seconds can hold

before that seraphim folds up
and becomes again
an ordinary hungry, ungainly bird
obsessed with insects.

ALMOND GROVE (1)

One morning you wake up and—
the almonds have blossomed.
Just like that!

Somewhere between white
and barely pink,
as if there were a thousand possibilities
along that continuum,
they arrive at the right shade
and stay there …

For a few days, everything is perfect.

Then the petals lose their grip,
never very tight anyway,
and the entire immaculate edifice
comes down—

the slow, snowdrift of its ruin
beginning something even better.

QUAKING ASPEN

Twenty years ago, or more,
we drove the twisted road once
to see autumn foliage
and never went back—
and never left.

The sunlight up there, unfiltered,
and the uncompromising chill air
cleared our heads
of certain dense notions
and gave us this image instead:

The leaves fallen so long ago
that never fell, but glow in our minds
like a nimbus, a holy light—
a light out of place on earth
in which angels would feel at home.

WHEN THE DROUGHT ENDED

The rain dries out as it falls;
only a few drops, brittle little diehards,

make it all the way down to the trees.
Determined—but hopeless.

I hear them slap hard and shatter,
knocking the dust off a leaf or two …

That was this morning. Tonight,
the rain has been falling for hours.

BEAR MOUNTAIN AFTER RAIN

You can live here for months and not notice,
unless it rains,
the vague mountains around us.

It's not just exhaust, ag burns,
and urban effluvia
drifting our way from the north:

Haze and smoke are both indigenous
to this valley.
Even Spanish explorers commented on it.

Early farmers, too busy to care—
like us—
kept their heads down and plowed.

But the last Yokuts anyone remembers
still looked up;
and every summer they had left,

climbed through the bad air
into the high country,
hoping to become invisible themselves.

URBAN REDWOODS

It must be hubris (as usual)
to plant redwoods here
where they don't belong

just because we thrill to see them
on road trips north—
green immensities with slab bark,

thousands of them, exhaling
so much oxygen
it makes us light-headed.

But here …
Their bark has turned dingy brown,
needles brittle, rusted like wire,

and if you could hear them breathe,
they'd wheeze—a death rattle
that lasts longer than we live.

TIME (1)

Sometimes we forget the sun is fire—
not benign light
but violent self-immolation
that goes on and on
closer to forever than our minds can think.

And during the heat of the day,
who notices anymore
that every innocent bush casts the shadow
of a crown of thorns;

or that everywhere we look
—if we do look—
we see posts and poles of all kinds
driven like nails into the earth,
which is dying too slowly
for us to care.

And when the sun goes down,
the sky bleeds …
But no one ever mentions that.

We're too busy—preoccupied
consuming our small allotment
of unredeemed time.

PEACE (1)

Walking the fields at dusk
with the dogs, my thoughts,
absorbed by thin haze,
will thicken into fog later.

The dogs, focused on
the rich and endlessly olfactory earth,
lope along solving scent conundrums
more complex than Hegel
until we startle a flock of doves
asleep early in a dark tree.

The birds go up in a heartbeat,
less whoosh than odd wooden clatter;
but before we've calmed down,
the dogs and I,

they've settled into another tree,
not far off, forgotten all the drama,
and gone peacefully back to sleep.

LIGHTS OUT

Now the moth can stop
beating his head
hopelessly against the lampshade,
and I can forget about words that won't come.

The frogs have broken their drums
and gone to bed;
an owl has finally put away
his precious old bassoon.

Only the insects stay up all night
to compose their haiku,
crumpling thousands of sheets of paper
before they get it right.

II

OJAI FIRE, 2006

We slow down and say nothing
driving through the burn,
too much on our minds to talk.

Hot spots still smolder.
Smoke clings to black snags
we used to call evergreen.

This devastation stuns us,
and it does no good to know
that fire makes things new—

cracks the hard seeds in us
so that hairlike rootlets
can take hold, impossibly,

and frail little perennials
no one has ever seen
will come up through the ashes.

WEEDS (1)

Maybe the weeds outweigh us
on the scale of ultimate worth;
and when we have all dried up
and blown away,
cinders on the scorching wind,
those insignificant little seeds
we sneer at
will open their hearts
to the earth again
and get on with it without us.

WRONG TURN

The wind must have taken the wrong turn
to end up here. Lost.

Now it's in a panic, spinning
insanely in the dust.

Disconcerting—if you look.
I keep my eyes on the road.

OLD COYOTE (2)

Walking along our own road
in the last light,
we came upon a coyote
that stood still in alfalfa,
watching. The dogs

wisely pretended not to see him,
and he ignored them, too:
not worth the risk,
somewhat quick themselves
with serious teeth.

But he looked hard at me.
Hard. And didn't blink.
In those yellow fire opal eyes,
I saw that nothing good
ever comes of human contact;

that if he were a puma
or I a rabbit,
a slight adjustment of scale
in either direction,
I'd be dead already.

Finally, he jogged off, indifferent,
having the sort of consciousness
that doesn't brood.
And then we moved on—the dogs,
for once, sticking close.

TIME (2)

The dust that never settles
out here on the Carrizo Plain
must be powdered bone.

No wind ...
Time has been around so long
you can almost see it,

though huge and formless, a ghost
with real teeth
that never stops gnawing on us.

KERN RIVER CANAL

Every river has good intentions,
even this one,
though it will drown you
for disrespecting its dark places,
its unseen, slithering currents.

It wants only to redistribute
the snow's wealth to dry flatlands—
an indiscriminate largess,
generous to thirsty crops in the summer
but without mercy:

The boy I saw pulled from the canal
had been trapped against a weir.
He looked cold and blue,
as if frozen to death
somewhere in the Sierras far from here.

RESERVOIR

If the thin remnant of moon
in the water
isn't visible overhead,

you must be dreaming,
unless you've slipped away
for a heartbeat or two

to see the old reservoir as it was
when you were here years ago—
or how it will be

some night not long from now
after you've gone
where time is perfectly still water

and all your uncertainty
like a vanished moon
reflected in it.

MOTHS

Hundreds of lemon yellow moths
out there in the alfalfa,
thumb nail sized, sketchy,

and much too restless to pin down,
are neither more nor less real
than all my vague thoughts, my conceits.

If one landed anywhere long enough
to blow on, it would dissolve—
dust rather than substance.

SEED

The summer grass looks frail,
old and so brittle
you'd think the wind would snap it.

But no. It gets back up again
after every gust,
much quicker than we do,

and shakes its empty pods,
going through the motions
that mean so much—

that mean everything in fact,
once the seed has been scattered
who knows how far.

LIZARDS

Like loose tongues that said
everything they had to say
and then some, lizards
sun themselves on warm rock.
Their eyes are self-satisfied, unconcerned.

When they see you coming
and skitter away,
it's less fear than sullen compliance
like punks on a street corner
when the cops move them along.

BUENA VISTA SLOUGH (2)

The heat bears down hard here
as if August,
scanning the landscape like a map,
has pressed a sweaty finger
into this place.

The muck green water hasn't moved
in months.

Dragonflies stick to the viscid air;
the birds have been stunned by it
and hide all afternoon
deep in the tule reeds …

This is where you come
when you finally get serious
about listening
to what silence has to say.

AFTER MIDNIGHT

A dog is howling somewhere
between here and tomorrow morning
across the fields
where farm workers live,
keeping him on a short chain
like their dreams—and ours—

not so loud that he wakes us
nor faint enough to let us sleep,
lifting his voice so we can know
how far loneliness reaches
before coming to the end of its tether.

WEEDS (2)

Here are the botched scrub brush
and miscellaneous junk flora

God decided not to use after all,
bad ideas scratched out of His notebooks.

At least I think so driving through—
until I see how evening light

makes everything invaluable:
seepweed, saltbush, mule's fat,

even the distant bare hills
where nothing ever takes root.

FLAT EARTH

Another ordinary morning unrolls from its bolt:
I've seen this fabric before, believe me.

It's the pattern with uprooted nut trees
on one side of a faded black road

and on the other, tumbleweed needlepoint
unraveling as the summer ends.

Who'd want to sew a garment out of that?
Just imagine how it would itch.

Maybe someone a bit odd—someone like me,
with dust in his blood,

who never really trusted those haughty redwoods
or Yosemite, that narcissist,

who wanted a flat earth, unadorned, nothing but
bare facts you can see from miles away.

EGRET (2)

Just before—just seconds before
the tentative mist turned to rain,
settling the dust
that hung in the air
all through a long, dry season,

an egret, wet and glistening
with its own intrinsic light,
floated down to earth so gently
it wouldn't have cracked
if it had been made of china.

Some things you never forget.

PEACE (2)

If even paper can cut us,
not to mention jagged metal, glass,
a dull axe, Mack's knife,
or someone's deceitful, serrated tongue;

if the wind and dead branches
conspire with gravity against us
to crack our skulls,
and we never see it coming;

if inward suffering without substance
—no blood, no broken bones—
leaves us shattered in a dark room,
can we say the Lord is our refuge?

Yes, if we are like the wild grasses
that always come back green
after drought or shove up through ashes,
ultimately invulnerable;

if deeper than any roots,
more compressed in us than life
in a seed, there is peace—
peace nothing can ever annul.

III

KERN NATIONAL WILDLIFE RESERVE

The unflappable mudhens,
those drab, disrespected stay-at-homes,
have nothing much to say, content
to float among the tule reeds.

Ducks make all the racket,
get all the publicity.
With their iridescent green heads
and panache, mallards come and go,
lifting off like combat choppers.

Black and white dabblers of some sort
run across the water, scrambling
to take flight from their false dilemma:

Anywhere north or south will do
as long as it's somewhere else—
and far. I like it here.

ANCESTORS

We had stepped over the slate wall
into high wet grass and daisies
to search for Mom's Massachusetts ancestors—
Brewsters and Hazens and such.

But you gave up and went back to the car
when the insects lit into us. I can't blame you:
nothing's meaner than graveyard mosquitoes
thirsty for blood among the dead.

I took snapshots and thought of other graves
on hillsides above rice paddies: your ancestors,
their stones swept clean for a thousand years.
Here, while Mom and Grandpa Charlie

tried to read something into illegible inscriptions,
the woods beyond easily absorbed their voices
along with sunlight, birdsong,
and a quick six or seven generations.

Westhampton,
for Emily Meiping

PEACE (3)

We all have faults to live with
that put everything at risk
and sometimes actual fissures
from which magma rises like it or not—
unquenchable, liquid hellfire.
It happens.

But places also exist where peace
flows unseen beneath us,
an underground river no one knows about
until it seeps up through the earth
as it does here
to form shimmering pools we can soak in.

Brewster-by-the-Sea
Bed & Breakfast

PENMAN SPRINGS ROAD

Everything is green now in mid March,
except the vineyards:

dark, worried wood still bare,
and not so much as a bud.

These deeply serious vines,
maybe with Calvinist roots,

have worked out the implications
of more than enough harvests

to conclude that grapes
and the wine inherent in them

take time … So they wait
as we wait to know

what love can be, aged in
the oak of unhurried hearts.

for Chris

BUENA VISTA SLOUGH (3)

If I take this dirt road,
dust will cover my car
in just a few minutes
as if it had been abandoned for years

like that rusted whatever-it-was
or the Whirlpool front-loader over there
shot full of holes.
Nobody likes a washing machine.

But if I take this road slowly
as I must—slow, reluctant,
and a bit disgusted
by all the dust and trash,

I may come upon a gray egret
like an angel rising
easily from a dead tree
and lifting me along with him.

OLD ROAD

This old road—like all such roads—
is finally breaking down.
No one uses it much anymore,

so the county no longer bothers
sending men with hot tar
to fill in the potholes.

Along the margins,
slabs have already cracked off
where sifting dust narrows each lane.

The yellow hash marks are still visible,
barely, once so insistent
that this road knew the way to go.

ABANDONED LABOR CAMP

The rusted out and weathered sign
has nothing left to say—
like wooden grave markers
that used to have someone's name on them.

You can tell that the two rows
of well-built bungalows
were tough for campesinos to get into.
There must have been a long waiting list.

But now, no glass intact,
and almost every door kicked down,
ripped from hinges that died hard,
the roofs slump, some already collapsed.

And the few shade trees
that haven't given up the ghost,
unpruned, unappreciated,
have gone crazy with loneliness.

HAWK (2)

An ordinary, dove-colored hawk
beating hard at the air

and brightly lit by a sun
not quite thirty minutes above the hills,

rises as close to straight up
as it can—which is almost—

then rolls over, spreads its wings,
and glides down and away.

What was I fretting about?

DOVE SEASON

The sun goes down earlier
—earlier, but not soon enough—
smudged by the smoke of distant fires
that burn every September.

The year has finished its work;
harvest is over, the crops,
like all dreams, sold too cheap,
and the fields plowed down to plain dirt.

In the last, dissatisfying light,
shotgun blasts like whip cracks:
nothing left to do, I guess,
but to kill the doves.

OCTOBER

I used to think the land
had something to say to us,
back when wildflowers
would come right up to your hand
as if they were tame.

Sooner or later, I thought,
the wind would begin to make sense
if I listened hard
and took notes religiously.
That was spring.

Now I'm not so sure:
the cloudless sky has a flat affect
and the fields plowed down after harvest
seem so expressionless,
keeping their own counsel.

This afternoon, nut tree leaves
blow across them
as if autumn had written us a long letter,
changed its mind,
and tore it into little scraps.

ALMOND GROVE (2)

And when blossoms come undone,
dismantled so that

the buds can get down to business,
petals litter the groves

(indistinguishable at a distance
from frost)

somehow creating a frisson—
a sort of shadow chill,

which if you didn't know better,
if you weren't looking ahead eagerly

through summer to harvest,
could be mistaken for nostalgia.

And what is there in us, I wonder,
that longs for harsh weather?

UNFAIR

Thin frost on the grass this morning:
the first cold snap
has killed
the blackbirds' little batteries.

You can hear them up in the trees,
already late for work,
trying to get their engines started—
tik-tik-tik-tik-tik.

Their yellow eyes must be
glittering with rage
because life is always unfair
and bad luck so arbitrary.

DECEMBER

All day the wind has been hard at it,
dismantling summer. Finally.

Leaves scatter across bare fields
plowed down weeks ago.

It's December now. Around here,
we have winter without much autumn,

recalcitrant heat persisting
like some sort of character flaw

this parched land can never overcome.
But we love it anyway.

PISTACHIO GROVE (2)

The old, ignored vines on the fence
have begun to leaf out,
neither first nor last this spring,
tentative, sparse, and a shade of green
that hasn't forgotten autumn.

The onion field beyond them,
planted last winter and slow to break ground,
is rife now, suddenly confident,
gun-metal-gray-green and so thick
the rows have almost grown together.

Between the onions and a nut grove,
a field of green wheat
has done its traditional dance all morning,
waving long scarves
with a hint of yellow in them.

Pistachios always hold back.
Hostile to anything easy,
they're still bare in mid April,
but when their leaves finally come
—and they will—

they'll outlast everything else:
loose-limbed wheat, febrile onions,
vines weighed down
by grapes no one wants to eat,
and even a hard frost.

SNOW ON ELK HILLS

Once in a decade maybe, the snow
falls here too, even here
on scrub ugly slopes where oil birds feed.

Not much. Just a dusting,
but sufficient to cool slightly
the overheated mind

of anyone who stops to look
long enough to see
that everything barren will be blessed.

STRANGERS

Solitary coyotes usually move on
when they see someone coming—
uneasy, though not panicked.

But once, rounding a blind corner
on a winding road
between one nowhere town and another,

we came upon a crowd of them,
two dozen or more,
scattered across a hillside;

and each turned to stare,
fearless, not much interested
to tell the truth—

the way we watch a stranger go by,
wonder where he's going, if anywhere,
and forget him as soon as he's gone.

DOWNSTREAM

The river is quiet here
and almost motionless, drifting
into little eddies of anticipation.
Cottonwood leaves tremble, excited,
although the air is still:

The wind has gone upstream
where you can almost hear,
if you listen closely,
white water applauding.
Something wonderful is coming.

www.ingramcontent.com/pod-product-compliance
Lightning Source LLC
Chambersburg PA
CBHW031211090426
42736CB00009B/872